31143011639516
J 977.3 Heinrichs, A
Heinrichs, Ann,
Illinois /

DISCARDED

Main

W9-CUD-193

U.S.A. TRAVEL GUIDES

ILLINOIS

BY ANN HEINRICHS • ILLUSTRATED BY MATT KANIA

The Child's World®
childsworld.com

Published by The Child's World®
1980 Lookout Drive • Mankato, MN 56003-1705
800-599-READ • www.childsworld.com

Photo Credits

Photographs ©: zrfphoto/iStockphoto, cover, 1;
Oleksandr Koretskyi/Shutterstock Images, 7; Philip Arno
Photography/Shutterstock Images, 8; Lotzman Katzman
CC2.0, 11; Charles Brutlag/Shutterstock Images, 12;
Alexander Gardner/U.S. Department of Agriculture
CC2.0, 13; Dave Newman/Shutterstock Images, 15;
MKE_railscenes CC2.0, 16; Pamela Joe McFarlane/
iStockphoto, 19; Tony Campbell/Shutterstock Images, 20;
Jason Lindsey/Alamy, 23; a2gemma CC2.0, 24; United
States Department of Energy, 27; Aphelleon/Shutterstock
Images, 28; Richie Diesterheft CC2.0, 31; John E Heintz
Jr/Shutterstock Images, 32; Everett Collection/Newscom,
35; Atlaspix/Shutterstock Images, 37 (top), 37 (bottom)

Copyright

Copyright © 2018 by The Child's World®
All rights reserved. No part of this book may be
reproduced or utilized in any form or by any means
without written permission from the publisher.

ISBN 9781503819535
LCCN 2016961129

Printing

Printed in the United States of America
PA02334

post card

Ann Heinrichs is the author of more than 100 books for children and young adults. She has also enjoyed successful careers as a children's book editor and an advertising copywriter. Ann grew up in Fort Smith, Arkansas, and lives in Chicago, Illinois.

About the Author
Ann Heinrichs

post card

Matt Kania loves maps and, as a kid, dreamed of making them. In school he studied geography and cartography, and today he makes maps for a living. Matt's favorite thing about drawing maps is learning about the places they represent. Many of the maps he has created can be found in books, magazines, videos, Web sites, and public places.

About the
Map Illustrator
Matt Kania

On the cover: The city of Chicago borders Lake Michigan.

OUR ILLINOIS TRIP

ILLINOIS

Are you ready to explore Illinois? Just follow that dotted line. Or jump in anywhere along the way. Whatever is your idea of fun, you'll find it here. You'll ride a train and paddle a canoe. You'll see dinosaurs and count squirrels. You'll meet Abraham Lincoln and the world's tallest man. So buckle up! Illinois, here we come!

WELCOME TO
ILLINOIS

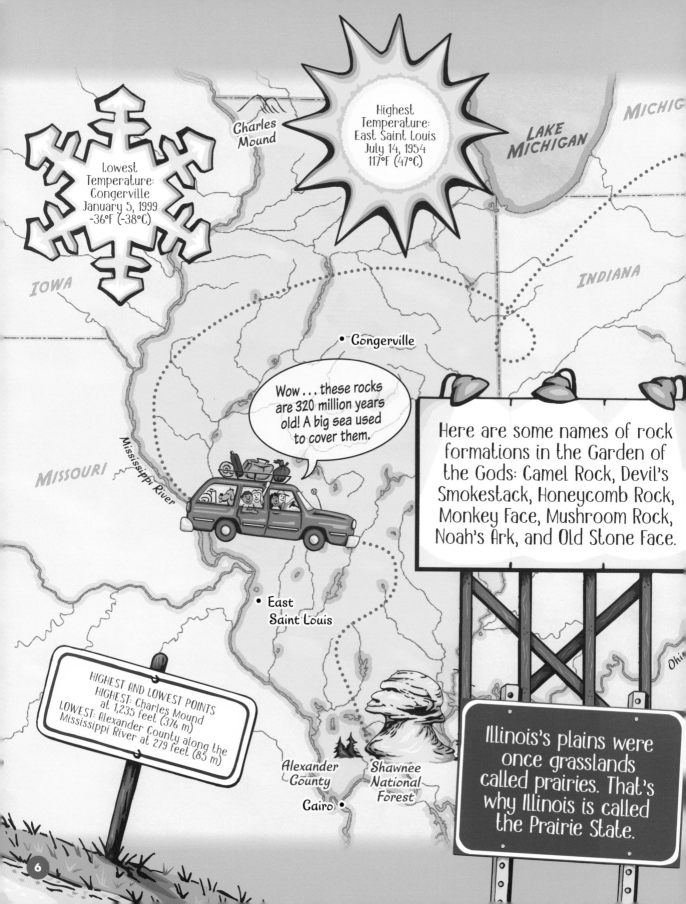

Lowest Temperature: Congerville January 5, 1999 -36°F (-38°C)

Charles Mound

Highest Temperature: East Saint Louis July 14, 1954 117°F (47°C)

LAKE MICHIGAN

MICHIG

IOWA

INDIANA

Congerville

Wow ... these rocks are 320 million years old! A big sea used to cover them.

MISSOURI

Mississippi River

Here are some names of rock formations in the Garden of the Gods: Camel Rock, Devil's Smokestack, Honeycomb Rock, Monkey Face, Mushroom Rock, Noah's Ark, and Old Stone Face.

East Saint Louis

Ohio

HIGHEST AND LOWEST POINTS
HIGHEST: Charles Mound at 1,235 feet (376 m)
LOWEST: Alexander County along the Mississippi River at 279 feet (85 m)

Alexander County

Shawnee National Forest

Illinois's plains were once grasslands called prairies. That's why Illinois is called the Prairie State.

Cairo

THE GARDEN OF THE GODS

Here's a monkey face. There's a camel's back. But this is no zoo. It's the Garden of the Gods. It's in the Shawnee National Forest in southern Illinois. All those critters are huge rocks!

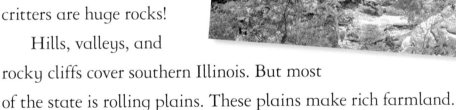

Hills, valleys, and rocky cliffs cover southern Illinois. But most of the state is rolling plains. These plains make rich farmland.

Northeastern Illinois borders Lake Michigan. That's one of the nation's five Great Lakes. Sandy beaches and sand dunes line the lake.

The Mississippi River forms Illinois's western border. The Ohio River runs along southeastern Illinois. It joins the Mississippi River near Cairo.

The Garden of the Gods has amazing rock formations. I spy a camel and a monkey face … Can you?

MONKS MOUND

Monks Mound is a huge hill near Collinsville. Cahokia people built it out of earth. It's as high as a 10-story building! You can't drive to the top, though. You have to walk.

Many Native American groups are from Illinois. The Cahokia lived 1,000 years ago. Their big city had many streets and homes. The mounds were for important buildings and ceremonies. A few were used for **burials**.

Jacques Marquette and Louis Jolliet arrived in Illinois in 1673. They were French explorers from Canada. They came down the Mississippi River in canoes. Later, French settlers moved into the area. Fur traders came, too. They traded with the Native Americans for animal skins.

Think you can climb all those stairs? A beautiful view awaits at the top!

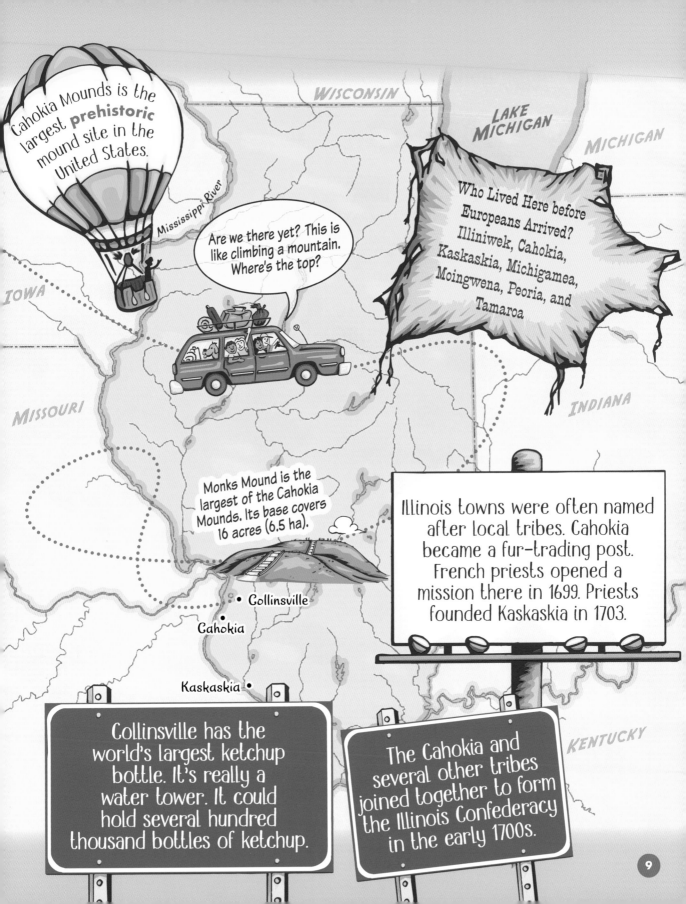

Cahokia Mounds is the largest **prehistoric** mound site in the United States.

Are we there yet? This is like climbing a mountain. Where's the top?

Who Lived Here before Europeans Arrived? Illiniwek, Cahokia, Kaskaskia, Michigamea, Moingwena, Peoria, and Tamaroa

Monks Mound is the largest of the Cahokia Mounds. Its base covers 16 acres (6.5 ha).

Illinois towns were often named after local tribes. Cahokia became a fur-trading post. French priests opened a mission there in 1699. Priests founded Kaskaskia in 1703.

• Collinsville

Cahokia •

Kaskaskia •

Collinsville has the world's largest ketchup bottle. It's really a water tower. It could hold several hundred thousand bottles of ketchup.

The Cahokia and several other tribes joined together to form the Illinois Confederacy in the early 1700s.

WISCONSIN

LAKE MICHIGAN

MICHIGAN

IOWA

Mississippi River

MISSOURI

INDIANA

KENTUCKY

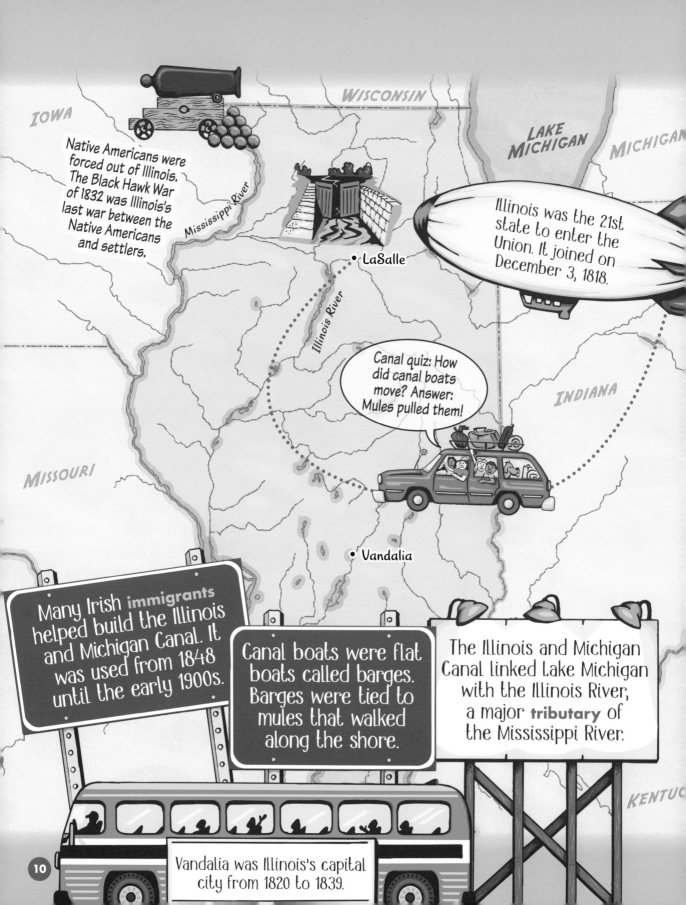

Native Americans were forced out of Illinois. The Black Hawk War of 1832 was Illinois's last war between the Native Americans and settlers.

Illinois was the 21st state to enter the Union. It joined on December 3, 1818.

Canal quiz: How did canal boats move? Answer: Mules pulled them!

Many Irish **immigrants** helped build the Illinois and Michigan Canal. It was used from 1848 until the early 1900s.

Canal boats were flat boats called barges. Barges were tied to mules that walked along the shore.

The Illinois and Michigan Canal linked Lake Michigan with the Illinois River, a major **tributary** of the Mississippi River.

Vandalia was Illinois's capital city from 1820 to 1839.

IOWA

WISCONSIN

LAKE MICHIGAN

MICHIGAN

Mississippi River

LaSalle

Illinois River

INDIANA

MISSOURI

Vandalia

KENTUCKY

LOCK 14 ON THE ILLINOIS AND MICHIGAN CANAL

Squeak! The gates swing open. Whoosh! The water gushes in. Squawk! The gates crank shut. What a way to travel!

You're watching Lock 14 at LaSalle. It was part of the Illinois and Michigan Canal. People dug the canal to make a waterway. It connected Lake Michigan to the Mississippi River. Locks held the water back. Their gates opened and shut. This moved the water to a higher or lower level.

Illinois became a state in 1818. Then thousands of new settlers moved in. Some raised corn, pigs, and cattle. Others worked in factories or mines. They shipped their goods on canals. That was much faster than traveling by land.

There are 15 locks total along the canal. Take a look at them all!

ABRAHAM LINCOLN'S NEW SALEM VILLAGE

You're hungry? Grow some vegetables! You're out of soap? Make some! You're at summer camp in Lincoln's New Salem. It's your chance to see how Abraham Lincoln lived.

Abraham Lincoln once lived in New Salem. He worked as a store clerk and postmaster. Later, he became the 16th president. He led the country through the Civil War (1861–1865). After the war, African American slaves were freed. But this was a long time before they gained equal rights.

New Salem is a blast from the past. You can even visit the store Abraham Lincoln owned!

Okay, let's say I want to be president. Is this how I have to live?

Dear Mr. Lincoln:
Thanks for keeping the country together and freeing the slaves. It's very sad that you were shot and killed. You might have done more good things.

Sincerely,
A friend

Abraham Lincoln
1809-1865
Springfield, IL

post card

Petersburg

Springfield

IOWA

WISCONSIN

LAKE MICHIGAN

MISSOURI

INDIANA

KENTUCKY

ILLINOIS'S POPULATION GROWTH

Year	Population
1810	12,282
1820	55,211
1830	157,445
1840	476,183
1850	851,470

President Lincoln issued the Emancipation Proclamation in 1863. It freed some slaves. The 13th Amendment ended slavery for all.

Lincoln's New Salem is near Petersburg. Lincoln lived near New Salem from 1831 to 1837.

Lincoln and a partner owned a grocery store in New Salem. Unfortunately, the store lost money and they had to sell it.

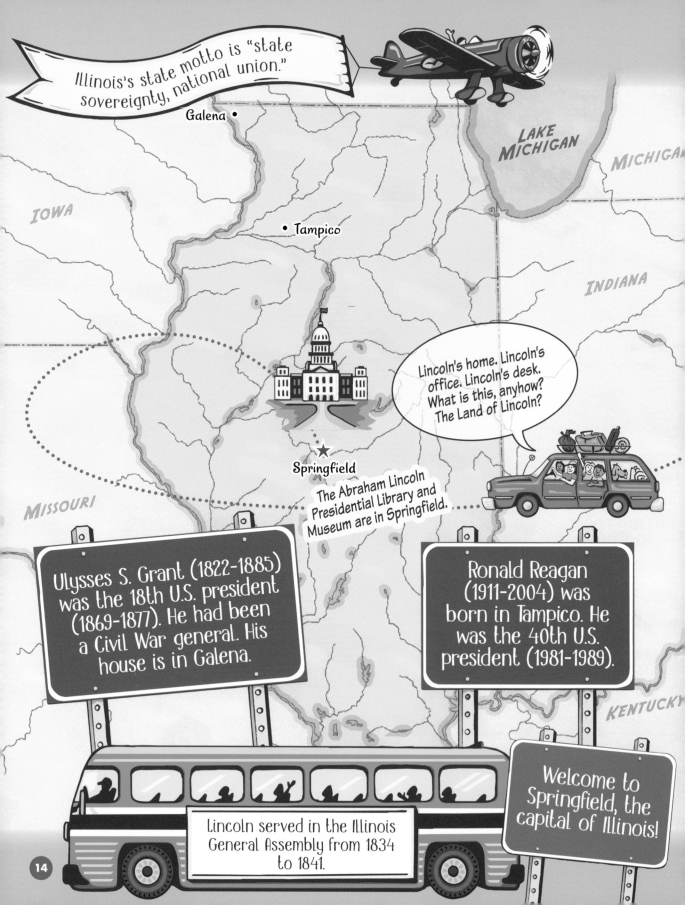

Illinois's state motto is "state sovereignty, national union."

Galena •

LAKE MICHIGAN

MICHIGAN

IOWA

• Tampico

INDIANA

Lincoln's home. Lincoln's office. Lincoln's desk. What is this, anyhow? The Land of Lincoln?

Springfield

The Abraham Lincoln Presidential Library and Museum are in Springfield.

MISSOURI

Ulysses S. Grant (1822-1885) was the 18th U.S. president (1869-1877). He had been a Civil War general. His house is in Galena.

Ronald Reagan (1911-2004) was born in Tampico. He was the 40th U.S. president (1981-1989).

KENTUCKY

Lincoln served in the Illinois General Assembly from 1834 to 1841.

Welcome to Springfield, the capital of Illinois!

SPRINGFIELD AND THE STATE CAPITOL

Illinois is called the Land of Lincoln. Abraham Lincoln spent many years in Illinois. His home, law office, and tomb are in Springfield. He also worked in Springfield's Old State Capitol. Now there's a new state capitol. It houses the state government offices.

Illinois's government has three branches. One branch makes laws. It's called the General Assembly. The governor heads another branch. It carries out the laws. Courts make up the third branch. They see if laws have been broken.

The state capitol took more than 20 years to finish. Twenty-two million bricks were used in the construction.

THE ILLINOIS RAILWAY MUSEUM

The train's whistling by— and you're on it! You're at the Illinois Railway Museum in Union. It brings back the days when railroads ruled! Visitors get to ride on a real old-time train.

Railroads helped Illinois grow in the late 1800s. Farmers were growing tons of grain. They raised cattle and hogs, too. These products went to Chicago by train. Chicago became the country's center for meat and grain.

Thousands of immigrants came to Illinois. Some worked on farms. Some worked in factories. Others worked in train yards or meat-packing plants.

The Illinois Railway Museum has trains galore! It's the largest railway museum in the United States.

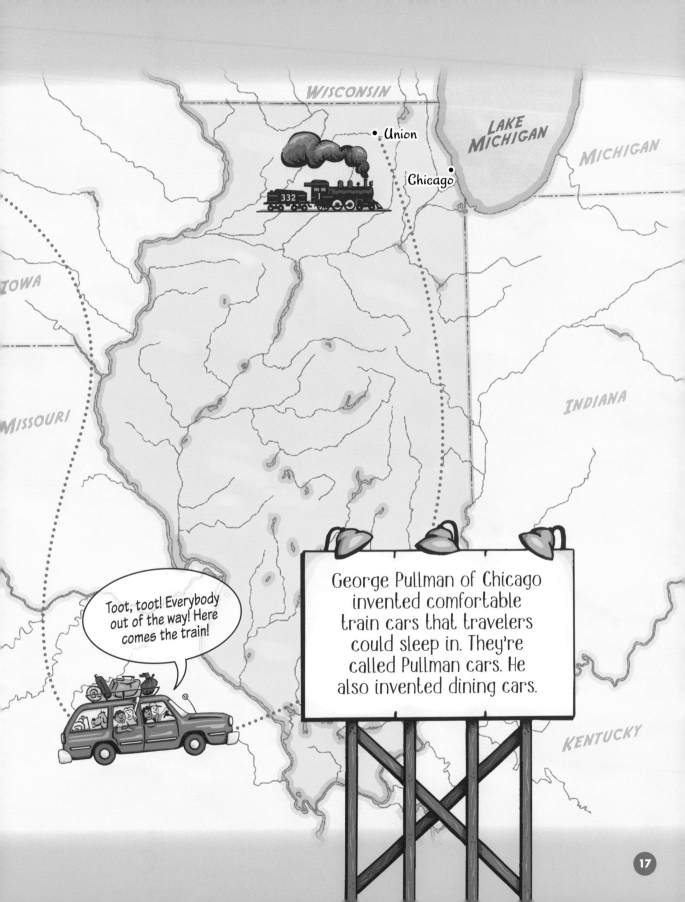

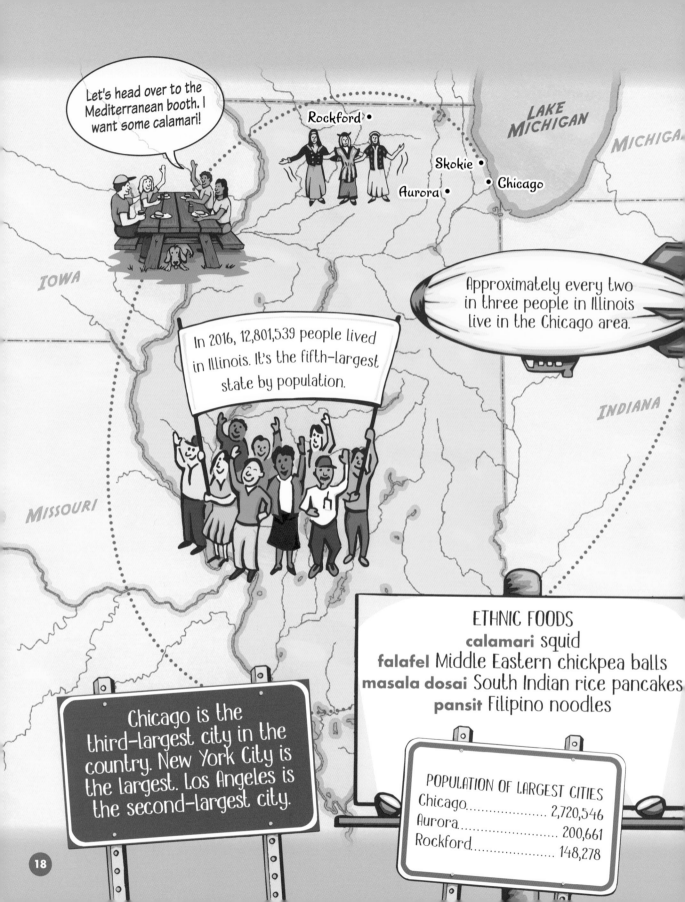

Scoop up some pansit. Grab a couple of falafel. Crunch on some calamari. Then snarf down some masala dosai. You're eating your way around the world. And you never left Skokie! You're at the Skokie Festival of **Cultures**.

Illinois is home to dozens of **ethnic** groups. They include Mexican, African American, and Polish people. Others have roots in Germany, Ireland, Italy, or Asia. It's a treat to explore their cultures—and their foods!

Sampling Middle Eastern foods is fun. Hummus and falafel are a yummy combination.

COUNTING WHITE SQUIRRELS IN OLNEY

There's a white squirrel. Write it down. There are three more. Write those down, too. And don't miss any! It's the yearly white squirrel count in Olney.

People in Olney love their bushytailed friends. The squirrels like corn, nuts, and birdseed. Some will eat right out of your hand!

You're more likely to see gray squirrels in Illinois. They scamper around the cities and forests. The thickest forests are in southern Illinois. Deer, raccoons, and foxes live there. Waterbirds love Illinois's lakes, ponds, and rivers. You'll find wild ducks and Canadian geese there. But don't try to count them. There are millions!

Some squirrels are white due to a gene mutation. Olney is famous for these furry residents.

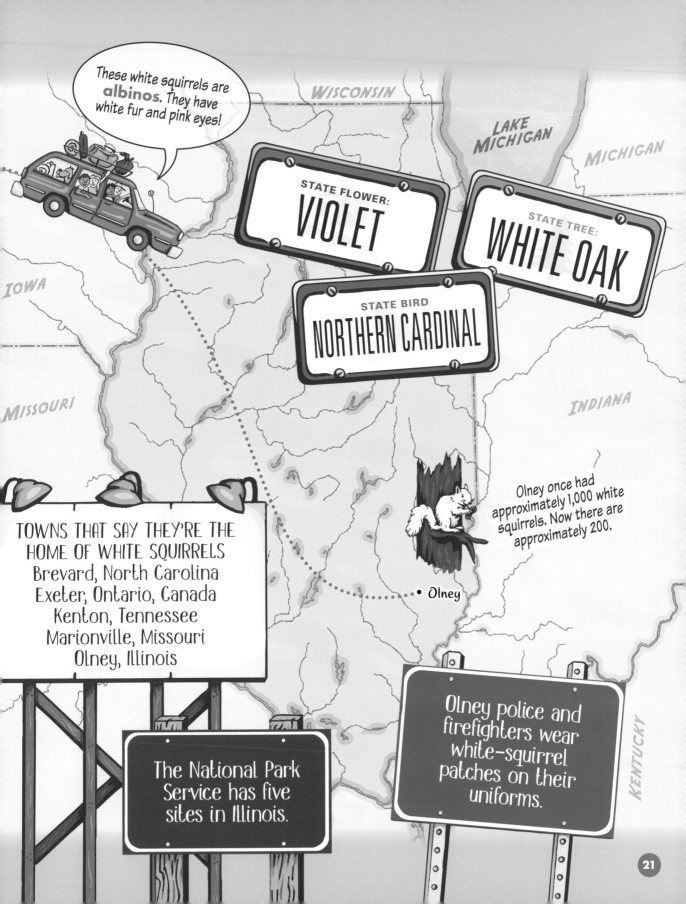

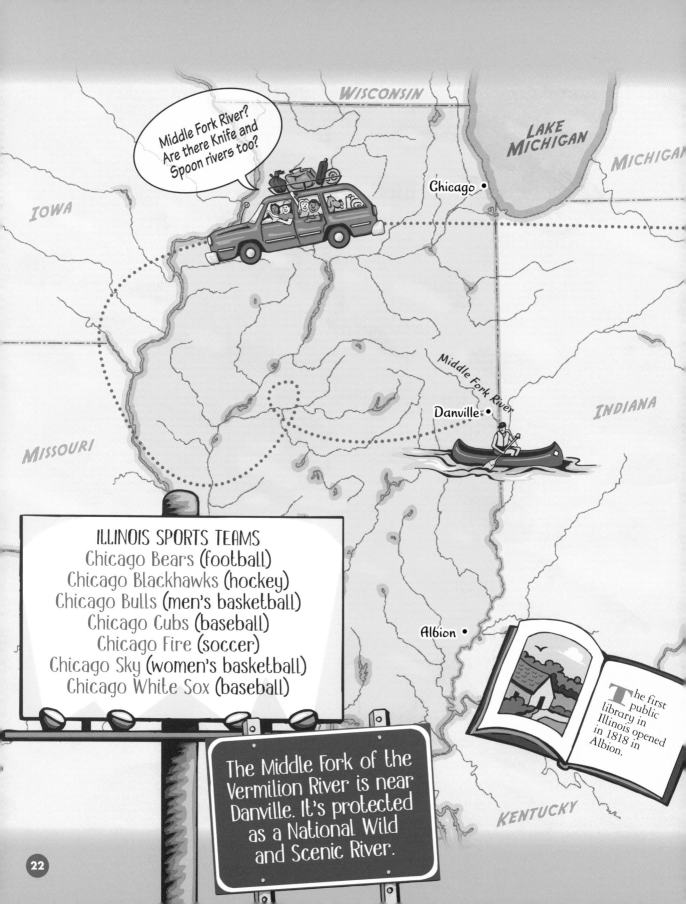

WISCONSIN

LAKE MICHIGAN

MICHIGAN

Chicago •

IOWA

Middle Fork River? Are there Knife and Spoon rivers too?

Middle Fork River

Danville •

INDIANA

MISSOURI

ILLINOIS SPORTS TEAMS
Chicago Bears (football)
Chicago Blackhawks (hockey)
Chicago Bulls (men's basketball)
Chicago Cubs (baseball)
Chicago Fire (soccer)
Chicago Sky (women's basketball)
Chicago White Sox (baseball)

Albion •

The first public library in Illinois opened in 1818 in Albion.

The Middle Fork of the Vermilion River is near Danville. It's protected as a National Wild and Scenic River.

KENTUCKY

22

CANOEING DOWN THE MIDDLE FORK RIVER

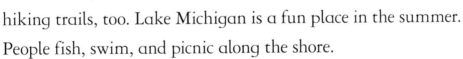

Whoosh. Swish. You're so quiet, the deer don't run away. You're canoeing down the Middle Fork River.

Canoeing is a great way to enjoy Illinois. There are lots of biking and hiking trails, too. Lake Michigan is a fun place in the summer. People fish, swim, and picnic along the shore.

Illinois has some great sports teams. One is the Chicago Bulls basketball team. Its star player was Michael Jordan. He made the Bulls world famous. Another famous team is the Chicago Cubs baseball team. They won the World Series in 2016 for the first time in 108 years!

Enjoy the scenic views along the Middle Fork River!

SUE THE DINO AND CHICAGO FUN

Chomp. There goes a **rib cage**. Chomp. There goes a head. Watch out! It's Sue, the *Tyrannosaurus rex*. She could chomp you in one bite! If she were alive, that is. Sue's skeleton is all that's left. It's at Chicago's Field Museum of Natural History.

Chicago is full of fun things to do. See a baby whale at Shedd Aquarium. Watch a sky show at Adler Planetarium. Ride the Ferris wheel at Navy Pier. Want to tour a coal mine? Or walk through a human heart? That's easy. Just visit the Museum of Science and Industry.

Sue was discovered in 1990. The skeleton was found in South Dakota.

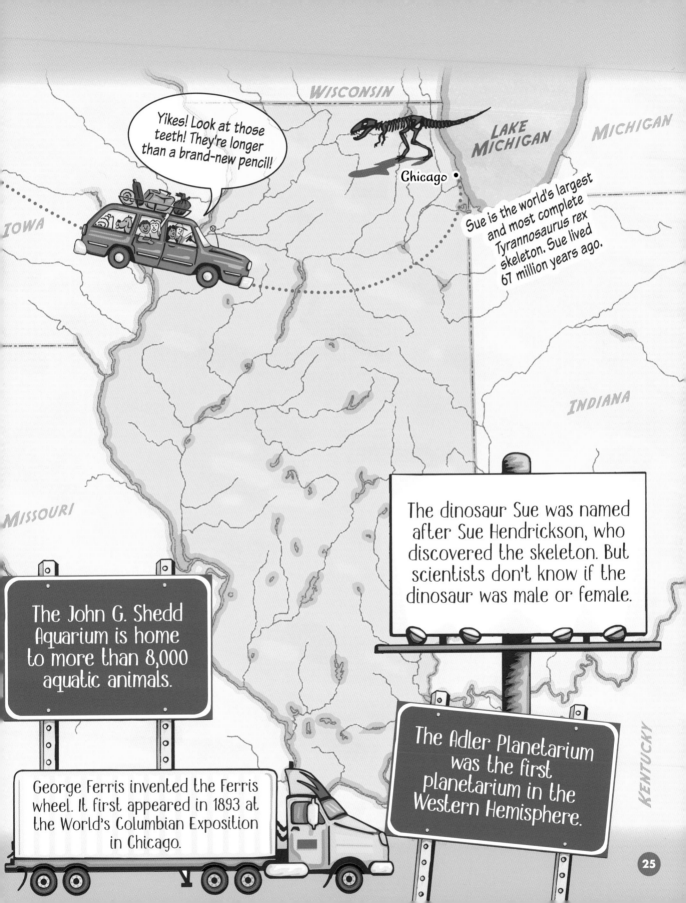

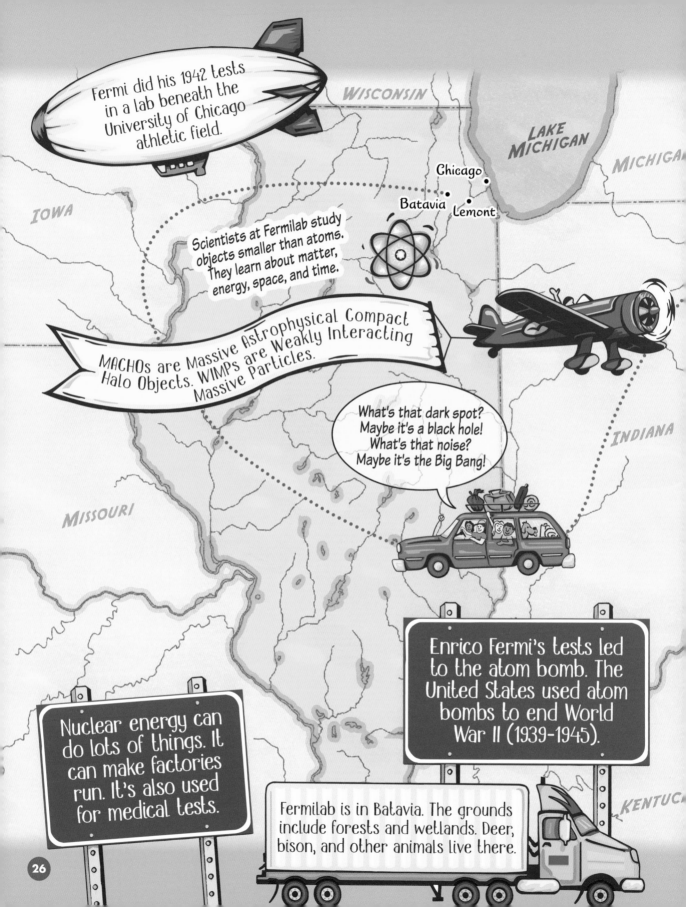

W hat are MACHOs and WIMPs? They're objects in outer space! You'll learn all about them on Fermilab's Ask-a-Scientist tour in Batavia.

Fermilab is the Fermi National Accelerator Laboratory. It's named after Enrico Fermi. He did tests with **atoms** in Chicago. In 1942, he produced **nuclear energy**. Soon, Illinois became an important center for nuclear science.

Argonne National Laboratory is another science center. It's in the town of Lemont. Its scientists study atoms, energy, and many other things!

Enrico Fermi is called the "architect of the atomic bomb." Learn all about his work at the Fermilab!

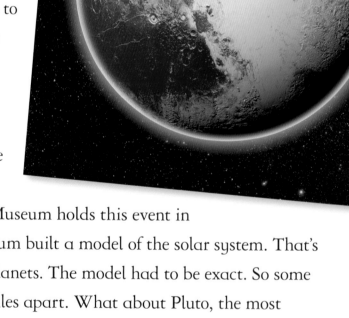

Hop on your bike at the sun. Ride to Jupiter and back. Almost 1 billion miles (1.6 billion km)? No big deal. How about a trip to Pluto and back? That's more than 7 billion miles (11 billion km)! No problem. You're on the Interplanetary Bike Ride in Peoria!

Peoria Riverfront Museum holds this event in the summer. The museum built a model of the solar system. That's our Sun and its eight planets. The model had to be exact. So some "planets" are placed miles apart. What about Pluto, the most distant dwarf planet? It's at a furniture store in another town! In total, the bike ride is actually more than 100 miles (161 km) long!

Pluto used to be a planet. Now it's called a dwarf planet, but don't worry—the museum still counts it on its ride!

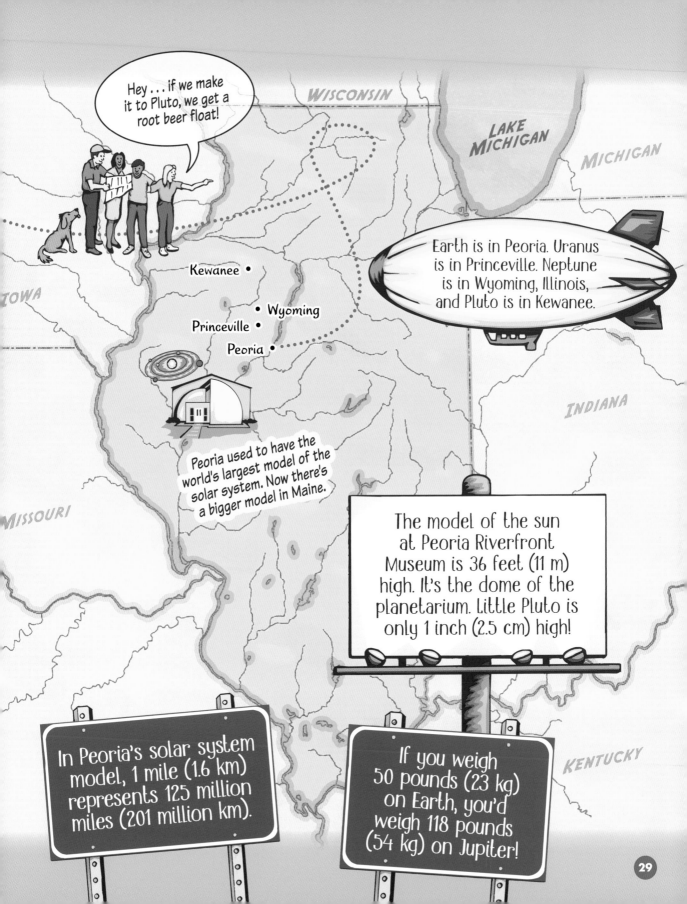

THE GREAT AMERICAN POPCORN COMPANY

W alk down the streets of Galena. Pretty soon you'll smell some yummy flavors. Just follow your nose. Where does it take you? To the Great American Popcorn Company!

Inside, you watch the corn poppers at work. You watch the coaters add special flavors. And you get free samples. Yum! It's still hot!

Illinois is one of the top farming states. It's in a region called the Corn Belt. Corn is the state's leading crop. Some of it is fed to farm animals. Illinois's hogs and cattle like it. So do people. Just think of corn dogs, corn muffins, and popcorn!

Like popcorn? Head to Galena for a tasty treat!

THE JOHN DEERE PAVILION

Are you into monster machines? Do you like tractors with wheels taller than you? Just visit the John Deere Pavilion in Moline. You'll see lots of farm machines. Some are gigantic, and some are very old. You'll also learn about farm machine history. Collectors can pick up some model tractors there, too.

Many Illinois factories make machines. Farming and construction machines are important products. Around Chicago, lots of factories make foods. They make baked goods, cereal, and other yummy things.

John Deere tractors are some of the most popular tractors in the world.

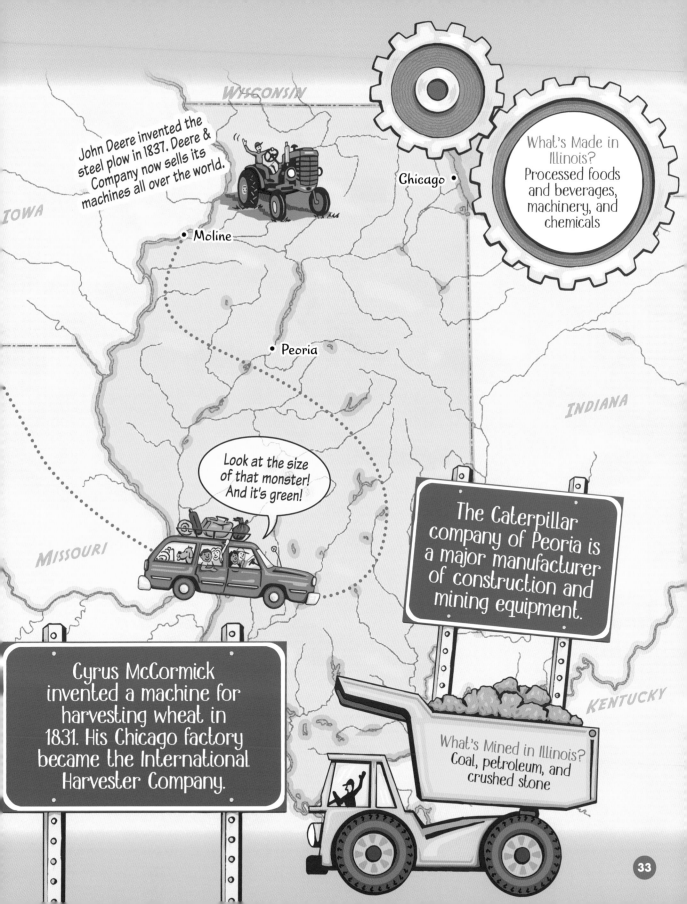

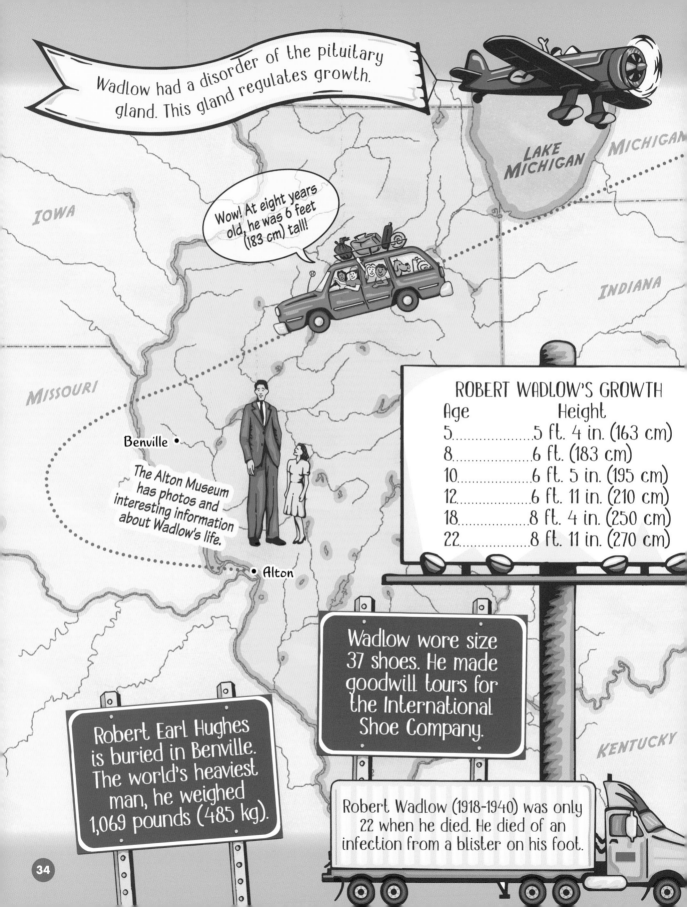

Wadlow had a disorder of the pituitary gland. This gland regulates growth.

Wow! At eight years old, he was 6 feet (183 cm) tall!

LAKE MICHIGAN

MICHIGAN

IOWA

INDIANA

MISSOURI

Benville •

The Alton Museum has photos and interesting information about Wadlow's life.

• Alton

ROBERT WADLOW'S GROWTH

Age	Height
5	5 ft. 4 in. (163 cm)
8	6 ft. (183 cm)
10	6 ft. 5 in. (195 cm)
12	6 ft. 11 in. (210 cm)
18	8 ft. 4 in. (250 cm)
22	8 ft. 11 in. (270 cm)

Wadlow wore size 37 shoes. He made goodwill tours for the International Shoe Company.

Robert Earl Hughes is buried in Benville. The world's heaviest man, he weighed 1,069 pounds (485 kg).

KENTUCKY

Robert Wadlow (1918-1940) was only 22 when he died. He died of an infection from a blister on his foot.

Stand by Robert Wadlow's statue in Alton. Your head might be just above his knee. This guy is a giant!

He sure is. He's Robert Wadlow. He grew up to be the world's tallest man. Robert was kind and friendly. People called him the Gentle Giant.

Robert was a regular kid. The only difference was, he was tall! At 13, he was the tallest Boy Scout ever. The other kids came up to his chest. He kept growing in high school. The other students came up to his stomach!

Robert Wadlow was an inspiration to many people. He is remembered as a kind person.

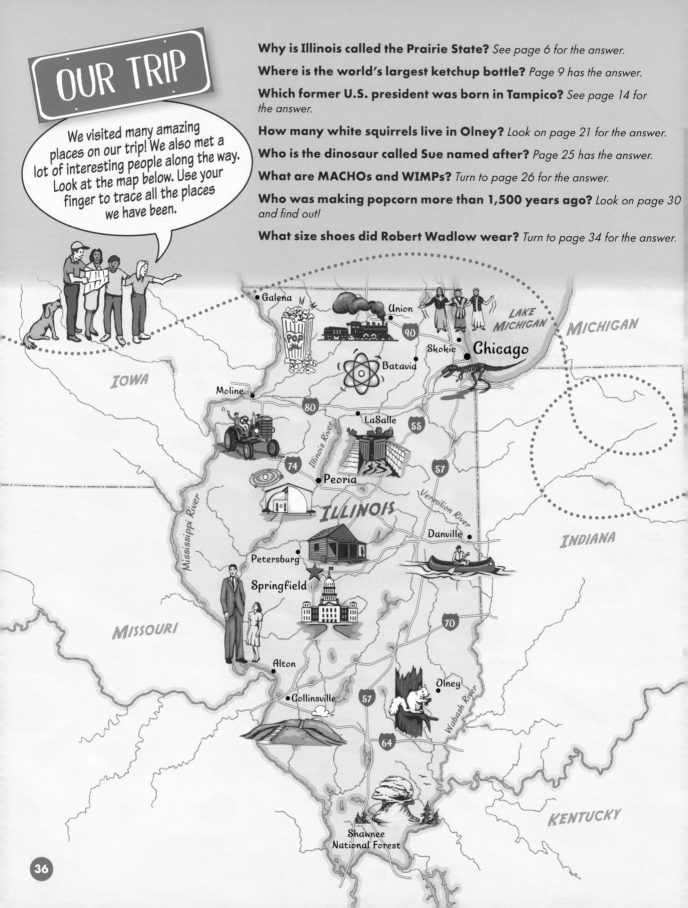

OUR TRIP

We visited many amazing places on our trip! We also met a lot of interesting people along the way. Look at the map below. Use your finger to trace all the places we have been.

Why is Illinois called the Prairie State? *See page 6 for the answer.*

Where is the world's largest ketchup bottle? *Page 9 has the answer.*

Which former U.S. president was born in Tampico? *See page 14 for the answer.*

How many white squirrels live in Olney? *Look on page 21 for the answer.*

Who is the dinosaur called Sue named after? *Page 25 has the answer.*

What are MACHOs and WIMPs? *Turn to page 26 for the answer.*

Who was making popcorn more than 1,500 years ago? *Look on page 30 and find out!*

What size shoes did Robert Wadlow wear? *Turn to page 34 for the answer.*

MICHIGAN

LAKE MICHIGAN

Galena

Union

Skokie

Chicago

90

332

POP

Batavia

IOWA

Moline

80

LaSalle

55

Illinois River

74

57

Peoria

ILLINOIS

Vermilion River

Danville

INDIANA

Petersburg

Mississippi River

Springfield

70

MISSOURI

Alton

Olney

57

Collinsville

64

Wabash River

KENTUCKY

Shawnee National Forest

STATE SYMBOLS

State animal: White-tailed deer

State bird: Northern Cardinal

State folk dance: Square dance

State insect: Monarch butterfly

State fish: Bluegill

State flower: Violet

State fossil: Tully monster

State mineral: Fluorite

State prairie grass: Big bluestem

State tree: White oak

State seal

STATE SONG

"ILLINOIS"

Words by C. H. Chamberlain, music by Archibald Johnston

By thy rivers gently flowing,
  Illinois, Illinois,
O'er thy prairies verdant
  growing, Illinois, Illinois,
Comes an echo on the breeze.
Rustling through the leafy trees,
And its mellow tones are these,
  Illinois, Illinois,
And its mellow tones are these,
  Illinois.

From a wilderness of prairies,
  Illinois, Illinois,
Straight thy way and never
  varies, Illinois, Illinois,
Till upon the inland sea,
Stands thy great commercial tree,
Turning all the world to thee,
  Illinois, Illinois,
Turning all the world to thee,
  Illinois.

When you heard your country
  calling, Illinois, Illinois,
Where the shot and shell were
  falling, Illinois, Illinois,
When the Southern host
  withdrew,
Pitting Gray against the Blue,
There were none more brave
  than you, Illinois, Illinois,
There were none more brave
  than you, Illinois.

Not without thy wondrous story,
  Illinois, Illinois,
Can be writ the nation's glory,
  Illinois, Illinois,
On the record of thy years,
Abraham Lincoln's name
  appears,
Grant and Logan, and our tears,
  Illinois, Illinois,
Grant and Logan, and our tears,
  Illinois.

That was a great trip! We have traveled all over Illinois! There are a few places we didn't have time for, though. Next time, we plan to visit the Willis Tower in Chicago. This building is the tallest in North America and measures 1,450 feet (442 m). From that high up, you can even see parts of nearby states!

ILLINOIS

State flag

FAMOUS PEOPLE

Addams, Jane (1860–1935), social services leader

Black Hawk (1767–1838), Sauk Indian chief

Brooks, Gwendolyn (1917–2000), poet

Clinton, Hillary (1947–), former senator and former U.S. Secretary of State

Davis, Miles (1926–1991), jazz trumpeter and composer

Earp, Wyatt (1848–1929), frontier lawman

Ford, Harrison (1942–), actor

Goodman, Benny (1909–1986), composer and bandleader

Grant, Ulysses S. (1822–1885), 18th U.S. president

Hemmingway, Ernest (1899–), novelist

Hickok, Wild Bill (1837–1876), frontiersman

Jordan, Michael (1963–), former basketball player

Lincoln, Abraham (1809–1865), 16th U.S. president

McCully, Emily Arnold (1939–), author and illustrator

Murray, Bill (1950–), movie star

Obama, Barack (1961–), 44th U.S. president

Peck, Richard (1934–), children's author

Reagan, Ronald (1911–2004), 40th U.S. president

Silverstein, Shel (1932–1999), poet and illustrator

Waters, Muddy (1915–1983), blues musician

Wells-Barnett, Ida B. (1862–1931), journalist, civil rights leader

West, Kanye (1977–), rapper

WORDS TO KNOW

albinos (al-BYE-nohz) animals with white hair, light skin, and pink eyes

atoms (AT-uhmz) tiny bits of matter

burials (BER-ee-uhlz) ceremonies to bury people who have died

cultures (KUHL-churz) customs, beliefs, and ways of life

ethnic (ETH-nik) relating to a person's nation or race

immigrants (IM-uh-gruhnts) people who move from their home country to another country

nuclear energy (NOO-klee-ur EN-ur-jee) a powerful force produced by splitting an atom

prehistoric (pree-hi-STOR-ik) taking place before people began writing down history

rib cage (RIB KAYJ) the set of rib bones around the chest and back

tributary (TRIB-yuh-ter-ee) a river that flows into a bigger river

TO LEARN MORE

IN THE LIBRARY

Duffield, Katy S. *Abraham Lincoln.* Mankato, MN: The Child's World, 2017.

Jerome, Kate Boehm. *Chicago and the State of Illinois: Cool Stuff Every Kid Should Know.* Charleston, SC: Arcadia Publishing, 2011.

Marciniak, Kristin. *What's So Great about Illinois?* Minneapolis, MN: Lerner Publications, 2015.

ON THE WEB

Visit our Web site for links about Illinois:
childsworld.com/links

Note to Parents, Teachers, and Librarians: We routinely verify our Web links to make sure they are safe and active sites. So encourage your readers to check them out!

PLACES TO VISIT OR CONTACT

Chicago History Museum
chicagohistory.org
1601 N. Clark Street
Chicago, IL 60614
312/642-4600
For more information about the history of Illinois

Illinois Office of Tourism
enjoyillinois.com
James R. Thompson Center
100 W. Randolph Street
Suite 3-400
Chicago, IL 60601
800/226-6632
For more information about traveling in Illinois

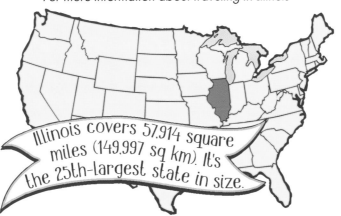

Illinois covers 57,914 square miles (149,997 sq km). It's the 25th-largest state in size.

INDEX

Bye, Prairie State. We had a great time. We'll come back soon!